THE ADDED POWER OF OBEDIENCE

Other Books by S. Richard Nelson

Turning Faith into Power

Gaining Power through Prayer

The Healing Power of Forgiveness

The Mighty Power of the Word

The Gift and Power of the Holy Spirit

Love: The Only True Power

Sustainable Spirituality

The Faith Factor

5-star reviews are a blessing to Christian authors. If you find this book inspirational, educational or simply enjoyable, please post an honest review.

The Powerful Christian Series Book III

THE ADDED POWER OF OBEDIENCE

By S. Richard Nelson

First Edition published 2014
Second Edition published 2019

ISBN-13: 978-0985247058
ISBN-10: 0985247053
BISAC: Religion / Christian Life / Spiritual Growth

Broken Hill Publications
Glenwood Springs, CO 81601

Edited by Stephen R. Gorton
Artistic Design by Connie Gorton

"From this broken hill,
All your praises they shall ring."

L. Cohen – If It Be Your Will

www.srnelson.com

"For God did not give us a Spirit of fear but of power and love and self-control."

2 Timothy 1:7 (NET)

Table of Contents

"I the Lord search the heart and examine the mind, to reward each person according to their conduct, according to what their deeds deserve."

Jeremiah 17:10

Introduction

"Your beliefs don't make you a better person, your behavior does." - Author Unknown.

There is an old Cherokee legend about a grandfather who is teaching his grandson about life.

"A fight is going on inside me," he said to the boy. It is a terrible fight between two wolves. One is evil—he is anger, envy, sorrow, regret, greed, arrogance, self-pity, guilt, resentment, inferiority, lies, false pride, superiority and ego."

He continued: "The other one is good—he is joy, peace, love, hope, serenity, humility, kindness, benevolence, empathy, generosity, truth, compassion and faith. This same fight is going on inside of you—and inside every other person as well."

The grandson then asked his grandfather: "Which wolf will win?"

The old Cherokee replied: "The one that you feed."

Two opposing powers grapple in every human heart and our decisions are usually influenced by them; either to do good or to do evil. The spirit of truth will always persuade us to obey God.

Obedience is not the requirement of a whimsical God who wants us to perform for His amusement. God wants us to discover that there are principles and precepts that produce pleasure in a planned but impersonal existence. We can, therefore, trust our obedience to authenticate our faith when knowledge and experience are lacking.

Mother Teresa stated that "God has not called me to be successful, she has called me to be faithful."

C. S. Lewis wrote, "Imagine yourself as a living house. God comes in to rebuild that house. At first, perhaps, you can understand what He is doing. He is getting the drains right and stopping the leaks in the roof and so on: you knew that those jobs needed doing and so you are not surprised. But presently He starts knocking the house about in a way that hurts abominably and does not seem to make sense. What on earth is He up to? The explanation is that He is building quite a different house from the one you thought of - throwing out a new wing here, putting on an extra floor there, running up towers, making courtyards. You thought you were going to be made into a decent little cottage: but He is building a palace." [i]

Our life on earth is about learning. It is about enlarging our experience and employing our faith. We are here to improve our perception of life's purpose and the magnificence of its possibilities; to savor the expectation of the promises of glory that await the faithful beyond this life and beyond all current comprehension; and to fully recognize that God lives and that He loves us.

But even Jesus, the greatest of all, learned obedience through suffering. (Hebrews 5:8). His hardship and affliction were part of his learning. Like Jesus, we are also here to learn obedience. We don't need to wander unfamiliar paths in search of truth. God has laid out the way and furnished us with the unfailing map of His law.

True happiness in this life and progress toward the glories beyond is achieved as we learn to be humble and to discard the constraints of disobedience to God's law. Isaiah invites us, "Come now, and let us reason together...though your sins be as scarlet, they shall be as white as snow; though they be red like crimson, they shall be as wool. If you be willing and obedient, you shall eat the good of the land." (Isaiah 1:18-19).

We all want happiness. We hope for it, live for it, and make it our primary goal in life. But do we live in a way that allows us to enjoy the happiness we desire so deeply?

The way to be happy is simply to believe in Jesus Christ and obey the gospel. When we obey God's law, then we can expect to find the happiness we desire. If we don't obey, we cannot enjoy the total happiness found in the gospel. To profess a belief in Christ and yet not enjoy the comfort and power of His spirit is one of the most painful experiences we can possibly suffer.

One of the most pronounced sources of spiritual power is obedience to the laws of God. Many are more than willing to die for their beliefs than to faithfully live them. The most effective way to introduce others to the word of God is not to die for it, but simply to obey it.

When God sends us a miracle, it is because we obeyed a commandment that justified a miracle. *Any desire we hope to achieve or accomplish that is exceptional, substantial, or advantageous will be realized through obedience to God's law.*

In view of this, it is incomprehensible how any faithful believer would ever choose less than what God has to offer. It would be proper for each of us to decide where we stand in connection with the primary and powerful law of obedience. We are always free to choose but we are never free from the after-effects of our choices.

Obedience to God is not an inconvenience, it is our ultimate aspiration; it is not a stumbling block, it is a powerful and profitable building block.

"Abandon the world. Run to God."

Chapter 1

A Law of Power

Today's world operates backwards. The things we should do, we leave undone and the things we shouldn't do, we can't wait to get started. The idea of obedience is a concept not eagerly accepted in today's society. Its appeal and popularity have essentially diminished, but not without reason. Satan has distorted the notion of obedience in order to add to our suffering. Many people have committed tremendous abuse by obeying unethical and immoral leaders. Others have been deceived into espousing evil objectives and have suffered the effects of blind submission.

Genuine obedience never has been blind faith. Rather, it is observing the edicts evident only through the eye of faith. We do not obey because we are blind, we obey because we see. Obedience is so essential to God's designs and purposes for us that we must reclaim it from irresponsible reasoning and inaccurate interpretation.

Obedience is a vital part of the plan of eternal happiness. No criterion is more critical to our well-being in this life or in the next. The ancient prophets and countless Bible verses all teach obedience to God's law.

Greatness is always achieved through obedience.

It is an undeniable declaration from God that everyone who is born will die. "When you eat from it you will surely die." (Genesis 2:17) Not a single one of us will escape death. But that is not the end of our existence. Our souls will continue to exist eternally.

Jesus was born with a mortal body. He was crucified but was raised from the tomb. He severed the clutches of death and rose to a newness of life. You and I must do the same. (See 1 Corinthians 15:22). We will go through the same process in order to access the glory God intended for us. We will rise from the tomb just as Jesus did. This is the purpose of our existence here.

Obedience to the laws of God is fundamental to that purpose. Stability, unity and purpose would not exist without obedience. Obedience increases faith and grants us access to the blessings of heaven. Rebelliousness produces only sorrow and despair.

What God is telling us is, "You forfeited My glory by intentionally disobeying Me. Now you must repent and stop doing things your way. I will give you another chance to regain My glory by willfully and implicitly obeying Me. Simply live by

My law of obedience and start doing things My way."

Our submission must be deliberate and intentional; it cannot be obligatory. God will never constrain us against our will. We must obey because we want to, because we have faith, and because we desire to please God. God always welcomes the willing soul.

The dominating ideology that links us with limitless power is the law of faith. Through our faith we attain abilities beyond our reach. The mind acts by reason, the spirit acts by faith.

Without faith, what proof is there that God even exists? Ancient traditions, sacred texts, and miraculous occurrences, however real they may be, are still only intellectual evidences and can always be contested. But through faith, the channel between God and man, the circuit of truth is established. Emerson declared, "Our instinct is trust".

As we obtain a spiritual knowledge of God and begin to understand the things of God, then the counter law is put into operation. Our knowledge of God makes us responsible to Him and invokes *the law of Justice*. His love for us brings us grace under *the law of Mercy* and we become debtors to him, and subject to *the law of Obedience*.

In this chain of laws each link is dependent upon the others, "For the one who obeys the whole law but fails in one point has become guilty of all of it." (James 2:10). If one link is broken, then the entire chain is ruined. If I, knowing the laws of

God, disobey them, then I will face justice. If I obey the law, then I will obtain grace, mercy and the blessings of God.

Our individual freedom is dependent on the condition of obedience. This is the great dichotomy; we are free, and yet we are restrained. "Take my yoke on you," said Christ, "and you will find rest for your souls." (Matt. 11:29).

We are free through Holy edict but become subservient to true doctrine by Divine decree. In trading this life for eternal life, we barter obedience for all we own. If we want physical power, we must obey the laws of proper eating and exercise. If we want financial power, we must obey the laws of economy. If we want mental power, we must obey the laws of study and correct thinking. If we want spiritual power, then we must obey the laws of God.

How do we reconcile the difference between these two conflicting ideas? Every one of us, no matter who we are, is restrained by countless cords, and eventually we learn that true freedom is found not in defiance but in obedience to righteous law.

I do not know of a higher law than obedience.

Everywhere throughout the world today we see signs of disintegration, disorder, and anarchy. We lack the cohesive qualities and moral principles that hold our society together. A dearth of love for one another and a disregard for law are slowly breaking down the orderly procedure of civilized society.

Obedience was the leading characteristic and the

fundamental principle of power of all the ancient prophets. We must recognize that this same source of power is accessible to all of us today. "Godliness makes a nation great, but sin is a disgrace to any people." (Proverbs 14:34)

When we begin to see obedience not as an annoyance but as our personal pursuit, then we will begin to see the power of God increase in our lives.

"The Christian ideal has not been tried and found wanting; it has been found difficult and left untried."

G. K. Chesterton

Chapter 2

Better than Sacrifice

To a people immersed in the ritual of animal sacrifice, Samuel daringly declared, "Certainly obedience is better than sacrifice; and paying attention is better than the fat of rams." (1 Sam. 15:22) The ancient prophets knew the power and strength found through obedience.

Jesus advocated obedience to divine law. The apostle Paul wrote concerning him, "Although he was a son, he learned obedience through the things he suffered." (Hebrews 5:8)

There are proprieties in Heaven different from the proprieties of the world that are instituted on the edict of obedience. Obedience comes to bear in every situation. It is the first code of behavior with children toward their parents. It is the first law with parents toward God and His ordinances. It is *obedience* that is better than *sacrifice*.

We need to possess obedience in our souls. We need to carry it with us day-by-day so that it will bless and purify us. The author of Proverbs in the Old Testament stated this very simply when he wrote,

"My child, guard the commands of your father and do not forsake the instruction of your mother.

"Bind them on your heart continually; fasten them around your neck.

"When you walk about, they will guide you; when you lie down, they will watch over you; when you wake up, they will talk with you." (Proverbs 6:20-22)

How much more does this apply to God's divine law and instruction!

Saul, king of Israel received a directive from God, through Samuel the prophet, to strike down the Amalekites, a sinful and corrupt people who opposed Israel as they traveled oward Canaan. The charge was for Saul to destroy every living soul, cattle, sheep, and anything that belonged to that realm.

Saul deviated from the directive and made himself the arbitrator over what part he'd comply with, and what part he'd disregard. He brought Agag, the Amalekite king, captive to Carmel and spared the best flocks and cattle. He thought he could justify his disobedience by making a sacrifice to the Lord in Gilgah.

When Samuel asked Saul if he had carried out the Lord's instruction, he replied, "I have done what the Lord said." Then Samuel countered, "If that is the case, then what is this sound of sheep in my ears and the sound of cattle that I hear?" (1 Sam. 15:13, 14)

Saul had to admit, to his dishonor, that he had not completely followed the mandate. He had spared the sinful sovereign and been swayed by the soldiers to seize the spoils to offer sacrifices to the Lord. It was under these circumstances that Samuel uttered the words:

"Does the Lord take pleasure in burnt offerings and sacrifices as much as he does in obedience? Certainly, obedience is better than sacrifice; paying attention is better than the fat of rams." (1 Sam. 15:22)

Saul's obvious wrongdoing appears to be that he made himself the judge in determining which part of God's commandment he should obey and which part he could choose to ignore. This angered God to the extent that He took the kingdom away from Saul and gave it to another. I wonder if many of us today aren't filled with the same irresponsible and unwise understanding that incorrectly influenced King Saul. Our great concern should be to demonstrate to God that we will listen to His word and obey His commandments even during the rough storms and trial we face.

Many of the possibilities and probabilities in life that are awarded through unfaltering faith, continued compliance, and sustained service to others may be lost to us during seasons of sinful conduct. And though we may be forgiven, chances for spiritual increase and advancement could very well be taken from us. Avoidance is safer than rescue. The power derived from obedience and the compensation of correct living are greater than the sorrows of recurrent contrition.

Abraham's example with Isaac should have been adequate instruction for Saul. Abraham was instructed to sacrifice his son on an altar. As heart-wrenching a task as that would have been, Abraham was prepared to make it. But Abraham received a second command, from the same God, suspending the previous directive, and demanding that he not harm the boy.

Abraham was willing to obey the first commandment. But had he then been unwilling to obey the second, he would have become a sinner in God's eyes. If he had disobeyed the *second* order and willfully followed through with the *first* order, he would have been a transgressor.

And if God appears to be inconsistent with Abraham or with any one of us, we should remember that His word is His law. He has the prerogative to pronounce one decree today and a different decree tomorrow.

We cannot justify ourselves in simply obeying the commandments that interest or appeal to us. It is easy to do what we already desire to do. But sometimes obedience to God also requires that we be willing to sacrifice. The sacrifice may be in doing something we don't really want to do, or it may be in *not* doing something we would like to do.

The things that we choose to do to demonstrate our faith is far more critical than simply how we talk up our faith. We should always try to do what is right, not what is easy.

The critical question becomes: What does God require of us? Obeying God is a choice we make. Each day and each moment of our lives we choose between the insufficient intelligence and power and God's infinite wisdom and power. We have as much right to the word of the Lord as did any of the Christians in Jesus' time.

"There is no fence to sit on between heaven and hell."

Johnny Cash

Chapter 3

Fenced In or Free?

From the moment we are born to the moment we die we are all subject to law. Parental law, civil law, military law, and God's divine law govern our lives. It is important, therefore, to learn the law and to live in harmony with it.

Jesus said, "If you love me, you will obey my commandments." (John 14:15) The skeptic will tell us that this is dictatorial and unreasonable, but all of God's commandments are for our advantage and all divine law is inspired by love and will bring ultimate happiness. When we realize this then obedience becomes a pleasure.

The students in a summer Bible class in Southern California complained that the commandments of God made them feel fenced in and trapped. They felt that the numerous laws of God took away their freedom. Their teacher took them to the basement of the church, to a large but cluttered storage room with no windows. Once inside the teacher turned off all the lights and then instructed the students to cross the room without bumping into any obstacles or each other. Needless to say, they couldn't go even a few steps without hitting something. The teacher then turned the lights back on and read to the students from the Book of Proverbs, "For the commandments are like a lamp, instruction is like a light, and rebukes of discipline are like the road leading to life." (Proverbs 6:23).

What the students had failed to realize up until that point was that the commandments of God do not fence us in. They shed light on dangerous and unsafe situations so that we can avoid them; so that we can cross through this world without bumping into people or situations that could be potentially harmful.

The principle of obedience is so often misunderstood. Obedience is a power that brings happiness into our lives and endows us with greater faith in the consequences of right action. It is said that "obedience to law is liberty". Real self-discipline is proven through obedience to laws that we enact on ourselves. Obedience to righteous laws based on correct principles is what leads us to an understanding of true liberty. Obedience to edicts that express ethical values becomes our Christian duty. Such discipline always precedes greater faith in the decrees of God.

One powerful reward for obedience is the development of a pattern of obedience.

We are invited to be disciples of Jesus Christ, to personify his nature and disposition as much as we are capable of doing so; to walk in his steps and to heed the law of obedience to God just as Christ observed it. We are not here to do our own will but God's will, in consensus with His purposes and standards. We came here to learn the inclinations of God and to follow the path that He has in mind for us.

God's law is in everything and is inescapable. Everything in this universe is overseen by supreme law. Henry Drummond tells us, "There is natural law even in the spiritual world". We can choose to disregard these laws if we wish, but despite their inherent elasticity which allows us a little latitude, defiance and rebellion necessarily bring unhappiness and regret. Regret is a powerful interrupter of our personal happiness and peace of mind.

The Ten Commandments, which the Lord gave to the world through Moses, create the foundation of all our society's laws. If these commandments were faithfully and comprehensively obeyed across the world together with the law of Jesus to love our neighbors, we would have little need for any other laws.

The laws of nature cannot be broken. We may attempt to overlook or disregard them; but we cannot break them. If we try to defy the law of gravity, for instance, by jumping off a cliff, there will be no avoiding the outcome of our choice no matter how repentant we may feel on the way down.

In the same sense, those who continually break the laws of God will be "broken" by their own indiscretions. Cecil B. Demille, the director of the epic movie, "The Ten

Commandments" explained that "men do not break the Ten Commandments, they only break themselves against them."

People sometimes get the mistaken notion that they are different from others. Some believe they can ignore rules that pertain to the rest of us. It may, at times, even appear that they are right in this misperception.

Some people disapprove of rules, limitations, or prohibitions of any kind. They suppose that defiant disregard for law demonstrates liberty and freedom, and they usually end up losing their freedom because genuine liberty can only be experienced through obedience to law.

God is not fickle or biased. He has no favorites. His laws are solid and unshakeable, and when we disobey Him negative consequences will follow. As we demonstrate obedience, we will always be favorably compensated.

It is very perilous to assume that liberty and license are synonymous.

Traffic laws are a good illustration of rules that are legislated and enforced for the good and protection of people and property. Violation of traffic laws often brings loss, suffering and even death. It's foolish to jeopardize our own safety and the safety of others just to show our independence. We can choose to run stop signs, exceed speed limits or drive without safety belts for the pure pleasure of showing off. We may even get away with it for a time, but eventually, if we continue to violate the law, we will surely pay a price in fines, injury, incarceration, destruction of property or even loss of life.

Countries all over the world have laws and regulations legislated for the benefit of their citizens. Those who disobey these worldly laws will suffer the consequences of fines, jail time or other penalties. Adherence to these established regulations brings freedom within the law.

Obedience to law brings liberty.

When we can recognize the significance, the prudence, and the need of law in a civilized world, we can begin to realize the wisdom and the power of being obedient. We need not fear the law or become slaves to the law because we acknowledge that freedom within law is essential to an abundant, happy life. Liberty is always jeopardized by disobedience.

Dismissive disregard of laws and conventions is irresponsible, self-indulgent, and unfortunately, often disastrous, while obedience demonstrates self-discipline and wisdom. C.S. Lewis stated that "Evil comes from the abuse of free will."

An obedient person is unpretentious and respectful. The disobedient are arrogant, contemptuous, and disrespectful. They encroach on the privileges of others to display their independence. Deliberate disobedience is juvenile and ill-mannered. Obedience demonstrates wisdom and insight.

Obedience to God's rules and requirements may at times seem voluntary but the prudence of obeying His laws has been proven through the ages. They are edifying and instructive; they are admonishing and cautionary; they require discipline and self-mastery. Although optional, obedience always conveys blessings, while disobedience bears its own consequences.

Obedience is the first commandment that carries a promise. Obedience is a form of honor; disobedience is dishonor. Obedient children honor their father and mother. Most parents would rather have an obedient child than empty words of praise.

Obedience is an indication of strength of character, disobedience shows weakness. When we are obedient, we comply with that which is regulated by authority; we willfully submit to equitable constraints. Most of us are willing to obey the person whose influence we value or the one who has the ability to assist or injure us.

Parents compel or restrain children for their own protection and education. A parent should hold back a child from crossing a busy street or from playing with knives, for instance. They do this not to flaunt their authority or power, but out of love and concern for their children. Locke said, "Liberty and indulgence can do no good to children; their want of judgment makes them stand in need of restraint."

Good parents recognize that guiding, encouraging, instructing and even expecting obedience from a child do not stem from a desire to demonstrate power or superiority over the child. Parental discipline is motivated by concern and love for the child. The older children become and the more experience they acquire, the more freedom they are allowed. And with this added freedom comes added responsibility. Freedom to choose and to act is an eternal principle, but so is the law of cause and effect. And so, God, our heavenly parent, gives us the warning, "a person will reap what he sows." (Galatians 6:7) It is because of His love for us that God establishes rules of conduct or commandments.

The laws of God are a safeguard and a protection, an assurance against privilege and prejudice. They apply to everyone, regardless of position, prominence, or prestige. When appropriately regulated, their rewards and retributions are unbending.

Repentance is a virtue, but forsaking sin is an even greater virtue. Jesus preached repentance but refrained from sin. We should live so that the need for contrition is minimal. Resistance is always nobler than retraction.

The human race will be saved if it will accept the law of God. Peace is conditioned upon obedience to the principles of the Gospel of Jesus Christ. Peace does not come to the transgressor of law; peace comes by obedience to law, and that is the message which Jesus proclaimed.

"If you love me, keep my commandments."

John 14:15

Chapter 4

If You Love Me

As Jesus and some his followers were traveling from Judea into Galilee, they stopped to rest at Jacob's well near the city of Sychar. They arrived at about noon and naturally tired, they stopped to rest awhile.

The disciples went to the city to buy food and when they returned Jesus was teaching a group of Samaritans. The disciples encouraged Jesus to eat some of the food they had bought for him, but Jesus told them; "I have food to eat that you know nothing about."

They didn't understand and wondered if someone else had given him food. Jesus explained to them that, "My food is to do the will of the one who sent me and to complete his work." (See John 4:8-34). Greater power always comes when we are doing the things that we ought to be doing.

Our digestive system is a wonder of nature. We put all types of grains, fruits, meat, herbs and liquids into it, and these foods are converted into energy, vision, wisdom, personality, understanding, bone and tissue, and dozens of other qualities that help us survive.

Something more spectacular happens when we feed the spirit. There are foods that enrich and enliven our souls and have a more powerful effect on our strength than physical food. Jesus made an important declaration when he said that we do not live by bread alone. We should appreciate the source of that power and learn how we can increase it.

Samuel said that "obedience is better than sacrifice; paying attention is better than the fat of rams." (1 Samuel 15:22) No other virtue compensates for obedience.

One reason why "we see in a mirror indirectly" (1 Corinthians 13:12) is that our eyes are not fully opened by obedience to God's word. Obedience isn't some ritualistic irrelevancy insisted upon by a capricious god. Instead, it is the condition of a caring Father who knows us and loves us.

What if Peter hadn't obeyed Jesus' invitation to follow him and become a fisher of men? What if Peter had chosen instead to think it over before he obeyed? But it was Peter who taught us that our souls can be purified by "obeying the truth". (2 Peter 1:22)

Jesus went to the cross for us out of a sense of obedience and trust. Paul reminds us that Jesus learned obedience by the things that he suffered. (Hebrews 5:8) Suffering is a hard way to learn. It may, however, be the only way for us to learn certain things. Insight doesn't come to the outside observer; it comes from being on the inside of experience.

When we can't free ourselves from the things which entice us and bind us to the world, we are not ready for the new experiences God has in store for us. Abraham's great blessings could not have occurred without his sense of obedience.

Obedience to a law simply means being in harmony with that law so that we can better our lives and make them more effective. By obeying the laws of aerodynamics, we have learned to fly. By learning and following the principles of optics we see through the vast distances of space or into the infinitely miniscule world of the microscope. By discovering and obeying the laws of electronics we speak and hear and see throughout the world. Science is a textbook of natural law and obedience to that book has produced the miracles of science we enjoy today.

As we discover and obey natural laws, we also discover that we can use them for our benefit. If we violate these laws, we suffer. If we obey them, we are blessed. We can depend on natural laws. Any engineer, doctor, or scientist in any field depends on the laws of nature. We can't ignore natural law and still be successful in life.

All the laws of God and all of the laws of nature are enacted for our benefit, comfort and safety. We determine whether or not to enjoy these benefits by obeying the laws and keeping the commandments.

Obedience to law means coming into personal harmony

with the truth. It is the most practical thing in the world. Obedience rewards you in whatever way you use it. If you build with it, it builds you. If you tear down with it, it tears you down. In obedience to law, you always reap just what you sow.

The benefits of obeying God's laws are beyond imagination. "But just as it is written, Things that no eye has seen, or ear heard, or mind imagined, are the things God has prepared for those who love him." (1 Cor. 2:9).

One of the most important parts of Christian religion comes under the heading of "commandments". Yet people seemingly resent being given commands. Ordinarily we don't like anyone who scolds us or orders us around. And when we read the scriptural accounts of some of the things that the ancient prophets said to the people who were getting off track, we may feel that they were being a little bit rough. However, this frank direct language has some important advantages. One is that it is so definite and clear that everyone knows exactly what is meant. Jesus himself was a very kind, gentle person, and yet he said some things to the Pharisees and others that were not so gentle.

Jesus spoke "like one who had authority". (Matthew 7:29) Jesus was never confused about right or wrong. He never speculated or guessed but always did what was right. His doctrine was tired and proven. When the young lawyer came to him and asked, "What must I do to inherit eternal life?" Jesus didn't quibble. He gave the only answer that could be given, as there is only one right answer – not a thousand, as we sometimes would like to believe

The story is told of a young engineer who was fired from his job. He asked why. The president of the company said, "You allowed us to take a course of action that lost us a substantial amount of money." The engineer rebutted, "Don't you remember that I specifically advised you against that action." The president said, "Yes, I know, but you didn't pound the table when you said it."

No one can accuse God of not pounding the table. He came to the top of Mount Sanai in fire, and with lightning and thunder, He gave us the Ten Commandments. No one should doubt that God means what He says.

How refreshing to feel the firm, solid authority of the word of God. We can absolutely depend on it. God is the same yesterday, today, and forever. He is not about to join some organization for the promotion of the new morality or for toning down the spirit of His law. The unwavering word of God gives us power and blessings.

"Lukewarm people don't really want to be saved from their sins; they want to be saved from the penalty of their sin."

Francis Chan

Chapter 5

The Blessings of Obedience

Joel Osteen teaches that "God blesses those who seek His blessings." There is an express correlation between obeying the commandments of God and experiencing His blessing. God elected to give to His children beneficial instruction and if we obey His directives we will be blessed. The opposite is true also; if we violate His ruling, reproof will be imminent.

If we keep the commandments and obey the law, then we can retain the hope that we will receive the blessings which God has promised His children. Justice, mercy and God's great love for his children prevent the sinner from receiving the same blessing as the righteous child who kept the law.

It is inherent that blessings follow, not go before, obedience. This does not imply that obedience is blind faith. It is, instead, a deeper experience of perceiving with the "eye of faith". It is affirming, "I will trust and try. I will do what God commands because he commanded it."

It is a significant concept of the Old Testament verse that obeying is better than sacrifice. Obedience lifts us to higher realms of behavior that extend beyond mere ritual. Obedience implies a readiness for immersion in righteous experiences denied to those trapped at the point of sacrifice and ritual.

In today's society, some teach a philosophy that we have a right to break the laws we do not agree with. This false attitude encourages anarchy and chaos. To the naive non-believer, obedience is an irrational submission to a foolish and recurrent burden. But to the faithful, it is the enterprise of the enhancement and expansion of the soul.

Obedience and blessings go hand-in-hand in God's plan. When we accept the principle of obedience we can then receive the promised blessings. Anything we wish to achieve or accomplish that is desirable, noteworthy, lovely, of good repute, that will be to our salvation will be attained by the principle of obedience to Jesus Christ. If today, we are keeping those commandments that are now in force, we are living a law, and our chances for glory are good. We are always blessed by obedience to law while transgression always brings unhappiness.

God's blessings are regulated by law. An unscrupulous and corrupt person may still be a good worker and be rewarded for obeying the laws pertaining to his or her vocation. But there are greater blessings than those which come from a successful career. We do not become good Christians by being good at our jobs. It requires more than vocational skills to enter the kingdom of Heaven.

Jesus demonstrated that complete obedience is found in following all the law that proceeds from the mouth of God. When the tempter came to him and asked him to turn stones into bread, Jesus responded that "Man shall not live by bread alone, but by every word that comes from the mouth of God." (Matt 4:4).

Some people question why they are apparently denied blessings. God does not mete out blessings in an arbitrary or indiscriminate fashion. Blessings always come by obedience to law. If we desire a certain blessing then we should observe the decree that the blessing is centered on. All blessings are obtained on the standard of obedience. A desired blessing might never be granted if we do not more faithfully live up to the law.

We need to be obedient to what we understand. When we accept ourselves as God does, we view our possibilities and our trials more accurately and we respond with the best in us. Considering the remarkable promises of obeying God's word, it's incomprehensible that anyone would willingly choose anything less than the best our God has to offer. Even a small seed of obedience will yield a bushel of blessings.

Our willingness to observe the law of God is a witness of our faith in Him and our love for Him. Ask yourself this; where do I stand in relation to the fundamental law of obedience. Keep the following four concepts in mind –

1. Do I study the Bible in an effort to know the will of God and learn His commandments?

2. Do I attempt to discipline my physical appetites?

3. Am I sorry for my wrongdoings and do I try to amend them by doing right?

4. Do I have faith in God even during hard times and adversity?

God's word vividly illustrates the blessings that obedience will bring and the inescapable anguish and misery of sin and error. Look specifically at the example of Abraham:

God was more pleased with Abraham's willingness to give up Isaac than He was with the sacrifice itself. For God, Abraham's willingness to obey was accepted as obedience, and Abraham was blessed as abundantly as if He had actually sacrificed Isaac on the alter. So God gave Abraham a second commandment, "Do not harm the boy!" (Gen. 22:12).

When Adam and Eve transgressed the law and partook of the forbidden fruit, it was as if the entire human race had fallen into a pit. We are powerless, through any act of our own, to emerge. We cannot climb out. We don't know how. Even if we knew how, we haven't got the means by which to ascend.

Our meager, human attempt, unassisted, could not bring us deliverance. In our fallen condition we require spiritual assistance. In other words, we need a ladder. The ladder that is provided for us to climb out of the pit is the Gospel of Christ. Without it there is no salvation. The example of the Tower of

Babel characterizes our condition: All our greatest attempts to reach heaven, without divine assistance, end in confusion and failure.

The gospel ladder leans against the rock of Christ's atonement – an act of grace and a free gift from God to all of us.

"My concern is not whether God is on our side; my greatest concern is to be on God's side, for God is always right.

Abraham Lincoln

Chapter 6

Not My Will

I frequently have to remind myself that God's will for my life often has very little to do with me. The Son of God gave us a supreme example of true obedience. Jesus, who is our example in everything, not only taught obedience but epitomized it. He said, "I have come down from heaven not to do my own will, but the will of the one who sent me." (John 6:38) In Gethsemane he prayed, saying, "My Father, if possible, let this cup pass from me! Yet not what I will but what you will." (Matthew 26:39)

Obedience is the key to the kingdom of heaven. Jesus said, "Not everyone who says to me, Lord, Lord, will enter into the kingdom of heaven, only the one who does the will of my Father in heaven." (Matthew 7:21)

Like Jesus, we can walk the path of obedience.

It is not always the easiest path. "Although he was a son, he learned obedience through the things he suffered." (Hebrews 5:8) We should always remember, no matter how difficult the choices become, that the end result of disobedience is captivity and death, while the reward for obedience is liberty and eternal life.

All things are regulated by law and no one is exempt from the law of obedience. There is no escaping it. Everyone must obey. Where the highest laws exist, we find the greatest liberty.

Our personal degree of obedience can be divided into one of three categories. The standard of obedience we set for ourselves will determine the amount of liberty we experience in our lives.

The three classifications are as follows:

The first is **counsel**. When we willingly take counsel, we exhibit the highest form of obedience and in turn enjoy the highest form of liberty.

The second is **command**. When we obey a command, our obedience is compelled -- more through a sense of fear of the consequences of disobedience than through a desire to obey. And postponing our obedience is dangerously close to disobedience.

The third and final category is **coercion**. Here we succumb to force and unwillingly obey a law because we have no choice in the matter. Our liberty at this point is relinquished.

It is generally accepted that the object of our existence is happiness. The highest form of happiness is found in freedom, which we experience in obeying law. Consequently, the higher the law the greater the liberty.

Obedience is not a senseless shifting of our individual obligation. It is a demonstration of our faith in a living God who will provide us newer and greater opportunities that will take us deep into the range of our own capabilities.

A rock in the garden remains in place through obedience to the laws of inertia. An airplane, operating under the higher law of motion, ascends above the clouds. Jesus lived the laws of loyalty and loved the freedom they guaranteed. In misery, Satan found himself obeying the laws of the lower regions.

The Apostle Paul taught that eye-service is rendered only when someone is watching what we do; as though our only purpose were to please others. Christ's eyes, however, are everywhere and therefore, if our desire is to please him, we must be faithful in "doing the will of God from the heart" at all times and in all places. (See Ephesians 6:6)

The servants of Christ, in contrast to people-pleasers, act out of a deep regard to the will of God, and from a desire to please Him "with all your heart, with all your soul, with all your mind, and with all your strength." (Mark 12:30) In this case, the principle of obedience is nothing external, but comes from within. It is an obedience which springs from the soul – from the entire inner person.

Christ's plan of salvation is not a difficult one. A plan was developed for our earthly progress toward heaven. We operate under the direction of Jesus in this process of progression. God's love is there to help us along the way. Our free will and our right to choose for ourselves are unending. We ascend or we fall in God's estimation by the use of our will. Our obedience to the laws of God determines our progress along this spiritual path.

"Remember that you may be the only Bible that other's read."

"Let your light shine before men in such a way that they may see your good works, and glorify your father who is in heaven."

Matthew 5 :16

Chapter 7

Beyond Obedience

Power comes from obedience.

The power that we seek today in meeting the challenges of a complex and changing world can be ours. We must simply stand, with strength and unwavering resolution, and affirm, as did Joshua, that "As for me and my house, we will serve the Lord." (Joshua 24:15) The idea of obedience, at whatever the cost, is the key to heaven.

Some people would rather regulate God's rules than obey His commands. But it is obedience to God's law that makes the way straight and the gate narrow, and only allows that a few find it. Too often our hearts are so much set upon the things of this world, and we love the honors of men, (that is, we love wealth, we love pleasure, we love this world, we bow down to it and worship it as Israel worshipped the golden calf,) that we cannot or will not lift our thoughts constantly in worship of our God.

Rebirth through Christ plants the principle of obedience

in our hearts and crushes the domineering power of sin, making us children of God. This rebirth is the Holy Spirit at work in our hearts, graciously inclining the sinner to repentance and faith in Christ; renewing our nature so that the power of sin is broken, and the principle of obedience is planted in our hearts.

Jesus' life gave power to His words. He showed genuine love of God by living a perfect life and by honoring His sacred mission. He was never haughty, puffed up with pride, or disloyal. He was always humble and sincere.

Led up into the wilderness to be tempted by the devil, when offered the most alluring and seductive temptations, Jesus refused to deviate from what he knew was right. In Gethsemane he exemplified the obedient Son by saying, "Father, if you are willing, take this cup away from me. Yet not my own will but yours be done." (Luke 22:42)

To Peter at Galilee Jesus said, "Follow me." And to Philip also He said, "Follow me." To Levi, the publican, at receipt of customs, He also called, "Follow me." And to you and to me the same voice, the same Jesus calls today; "Follow me."

Are we willing to obey?

What can we do for ourselves? What acts of obedience are required of us? What can we do to benefit from what Jesus has done in our behalf?

The ladder has been lowered into the pit. How do we take advantage of the divine assistance Jesus is offering us?

The answer is simple: We must climb. Without a ladder,

we could never ascend out of this pit. All our cleverness and ability would not help us. But now, given the means through Jesus Christ, our Savior, we can climb from earth to heaven, rung by rung.

Some want to believe that the gospel is like a cafeteria, where we take what we want and leave the rest. But if we do things God's way only when it is convenient, we are not obeying God. If we obey only some of the Ten Commandments, we are not truly obeying the Ten Commandments.

If obeying God's law meant keeping only one commandment, what would that commandment be? Jesus answered that question for us when asked, "Teacher, which commandment in the law is the greatest?

"Jesus said to him, Love the Lord your God with all your heart, with all your soul, and with all your mind. This is the first and greatest commandment. The second is like it, Love your neighbor as yourself." (Matt. 22:36-39)

The other laws are all based on these two commandments. The law of obedience is based on love of God: "If you love me, you will obey my commandments." (John 14:15) The other laws of God are meant to teach us to love each other. Love is what God is all about.

Obeying God is not difficult when we do it out of love for Him who has so graciously blessed us. Jesus asked us to "take my yoke on you and learn from me; because I am gentle and humble in heart, and you will find rest for your souls.

"For my yoke is easy to bear, and my load is not hard to carry." (Matt. 11:29-30)

Just as a patient cannot accept a doctor and at the same time, reject his remedy, so we cannot accept Christ into our hearts and yet refuse to obey his laws. Spiritual power and stability are acquired only from persistent obedience to God's laws.

5-star reviews are like a blessing sent from heaven for Christian authors. If you found this book to be inspirational, uplifting or simply enjoyable, please post an honest review.

About the Author

Rich Nelson is the author of a variety of published articles on topics such as religious education, family values, health, and politics. His work has appeared in *Christian Education Today, Church Teacher, Parish Teacher, Living with Teenagers, Liberty Magazine,* and many others.

Contact Information:

Broken Hill Christian Publications

Glenwood Springs, CO 91601

Email Rich at: rich@srnelson.com

Visit Rich at: www.srnelson.com

Other Books by Rich Nelson

Turning Faith into Power

Book 1 in The Powerful Christian Series.

Turning Faith into Power is the first in a series of instructive and inspirational books from The Powerful Christian Series by S. Richard Nelson. The Savior says in Matthew 17:19-20, "For most assuredly I tell you, If you have faith as a grain of mustard seed, you will tell this mountain, move from here to there, and it will move; and nothing will be impossible to you."

What mountains would you remove from your life if you had the faith of a mustard seed?

What's stopping you from removing the obstacles in your life?

Do you utilize your faith as a principle of action and power?

Is your faith centered where it will be most effective?

Do you have adequate faith in yourself?

As believing Christians there is substantial power available to us. It is the power of faith. Through the bounteous mercy and love of Jesus Christ we receive his grace - a divine means of strength. The power available to us through Jesus Christ is very real.

Gaining Power through Prayer

Book 2 in The Powerful Christian Series

Sincere prayer is a fountain of divine power flowing into our lives. Through prayer we gain clear and precise direction. Through prayer we access the strength of character to perform God's will – to do what is right. Prayer is the process we use to place ourselves in contact with God.

The impressive power of prayer warrants the consideration not only of Christians, but of all societies. This little booklet highlights the principle applications and purposes of prayer. It confirms that God does answer our prayers and demonstrates how we can be more aware of those divine answers. It also examines the challenging question of why, at times, it appears that God does not answer us and what we can do about it.

Excerpt from

The Healing Power of Forgiveness

Book 4 in
The Powerful Christian Series

by S. Richard Nelson

available at www.srnelson.com

Excerpt:

The Healing Power of Forgiveness

Repentance and forgiveness are the essence of the gospel of Jesus Christ. They are principles that offer hope, expectation and encouragement to every believer. As mortal humans living in a world of endless temptations and enticements, we can very easily make mistakes and commit sins. The atonement effected by Jesus Christ assures us that our slip-ups and missteps may be resolved through godly sorrow and by turning from our unrighteous ways.

The great blessing and miracle is that you and I, human and flawed as we are, have the very same power given to us. It is this inner power of forgiveness that changes lives. We are most like Jesus Christ when we forgive another person....

Forgiving others is often the hardest thing required of us by the gospel of Jesus Christ. Although it is sometimes difficult to implement, forgiveness is fundamental to peace in personal relationships.

As one unknown author explains: "The first to apologize is the bravest; the first to forgive is the strongest; the first to forget is the happiest."

We have a responsibility and obligation as followers of Jesus Christ to exercise the power of mercy and forgiveness toward others. Just as we receive forgiveness through faith on Jesus Christ, it is also through our faith that we can have the power to forgive others. All of which can be summed up in a single word—grace....

The process of forgiving another person often may require a seemingly unsurmountable effort but forgiveness is always the sure and reliable path to peace and healing. If you feel that you have been seriously wronged, if you are an innocent victim, don't harbor feelings of anger or hatred at the injustice. Honestly and sincerely forgive. (Mark 11:25)

If your offender requires discipline for a serious transgression against you, let the proper civil authorities handle the punishment and correction. Don't burden your own life with thoughts of retribution. God's mill of justice may grind slowly, but it grinds exceedingly well. No one will escape the consequences of the violation of God's laws. In His own time and in His own way, a full payment will be exacted for every unrepented evil act others commit against you.

Jesus' plea for us to stop hanging on to the sins of others in no way lessens the gravity of what the initial sinner did. And yet, He expects us to forgive so that when we need it, His forgiveness will also be available for us.

Forgiveness of that type is never easy or immediate. Depending on the gravity of the injustice, it might initially seem unattainable. But it isn't unattainable, or the Lord wouldn't have asked us to do it. I believe Christ is serious when He tells us to forgive others. He gave us His words because He means them. He is the ultimate example of saying what He means and meaning what He says. He has commanded us to forgive everyone! We need to find a way, and, if we ask, He will help us find that way....

We might sometimes think that Jesus' counsel of loving our enemies, blessing those that curse us, doing good to those that hate us, and praying for those that despitefully use and persecute us as being merely something to discuss in Sunday School but with little value for life's actual situations. But this is not so. In these few sentences Jesus has outlined a philosophy of human relations that provides us with one of the finest codes of conduct ever put into words. When we accept this philosophy, we are given a substantial advantage in life. On the other hand, if we reject Jesus' counsel and fail to make this beneficial philosophy a part of us, we suffer a serious loss in life.

Once we have accepted Christ into our hearts and had our sins forgiven, we retain that forgiveness by forgiving others and by a lifetime commitment of charitable conduct. Returning to our sinful selves after our initial remission of sins is comparable to the return of leukemic blood cells after the initial remission of the disease. Leukemia is a malignant disease caused by the uncontrolled growth of leukocyte precursors in blood, bone marrow and certain body tissues. Proper treatment will often bring this life-threatening disease into remission, eliminating the cancerous, malignant blood cells.

Much of the world today suffers from a spiritual leukemia. The diffusion of sin destroys the soul just like the dissemination of leukemic blood cells destroys the body. The spread of sinful conduct in our lives can be brought into remission when we accept Christ. Our new state of spiritual well-being requires that we forsake sin and embrace righteousness.

[i] Lewis, C.S., Mere Christianity, New York: Macmillan Publishing Co., Inc., Macmillan Paperbacks Edition, 1960, p. 174.

www.ingramcontent.com/pod-product-compliance
Lightning Source LLC
Chambersburg PA
CBHW060650030426

42337CB00017B/2535